In the Rustling Grass

In the Rustling Grass

By

HERBERT F. BROKERING

Photographs by

Sister Noemi

AUGSBURG PUBLISHING HOUSE
Minneapolis, Minnesota

Scripture quotations are from the Revised Standard Version of the
Bible, copyright 1946 and 1952 by the Division of Christian Edu-
cation of the National Council of Churches.

The quotation "This is my Father's world" is from *Thoughts for
Everyday Living* by Maltbie D. Babcock, copyright 1901 Charles
Scribner's Sons.

Manufactured in the United States of America

This is my Father's world,
   And to my listening ears
All nature sings, and round me rings
   The music of the spheres.
This is my Father's world;
   I rest me in the thought
Of rocks and trees, of skies and seas,
   His hand the wonders wrought.

This is my Father's world;
   The birds their carols raise;
The morning light, the lily white,
   Declare their Maker's praise.
This is my Father's world;
   He shines in all that's fair;
In the rustling grass I hear him pass,
   He speaks to me everywhere.

This is my Father's world,
   O let me ne'er forget
That though the wrong seems oft so strong,
   God is the Ruler yet.
This is my Father's world;
   Why should my heart be sad?
The Lord is King, let the heavens ring;
   God reigns, let the earth be glad!

Maltbie D. Babcock

Chorals began with angels
gathered to sing from heaven above
to the earth.
All contain the same pure text.
They pitched their voices
and pointed their notes
manward.
Mortal translations
of their lyrics
covered the fields
and stirred the shepherds.
Later they awoke Joseph in a dream.
On the first day of the week
they filled the ears of visitors to the tomb.
In the imagination of the heart
there are new melodies
and new texts,
but all these are modern versions
of the old angel choral
titled
Glory to God,
good will to man.

To the only wise God
be glory . . .
Romans 16:27

Out of the fruit of the earth
God raised up a Savior.
In the womb
of the woman in Nazareth
lay curled
the Child
and Christ.
The earth now held
the Messiah.
Heaven
and earth
and one woman
were synchronized
for an event
clocking both time and eternity.
While the mother
cuddled the Child
her lips received the Magnificat
and her people received
a Good Shepherd,
named Jesus,
Savior from sin.
Earth needed such a Shepherd
with a fitting crozier.

And she gave birth
to her first-born son . . .
Luke 2:7

The sky was ablaze
with glory
and joy
as angels tumbled their glorias
earthward
which moved like a thousand strings
of harps and lyres
to premiere peace,
now famous in all tongues.
Sheer illumination.
Glory had burst
into sprays and splashes.
Sky and hillside,
heaven and earth,
were enmeshed
in light
and joy
and glory
and God's will.
The earth was ripe
for him.

Glory to God . . .
Luke 2:13

With heads bowed
the shepherds looked down
on the Child.
In tense reverence
they were fixed with adoration.
Each was clothed in belief
and trust.
They stood delicate,
lest this surprise
be a desert mirage.
It was a new beginning
for the shepherds
who were glad
that they had believed their ears
and eyes
and prophecies.

They went with haste,
and found Mary and Joseph,
and the babe
lying in the manger . . .
Luke 2:16

A seed on the wood steps
is like the Child on the hay.
It is a greater event
than the naked eye can see.
The tiny seed
that pauses long enough
to be studied
and described
calls to memory him
who was on earth long enough
to be known
and described by man.
Seed is life.
He is life.
To be reminded of him
by a seed on a wood step
is to have a quick Christmas.
It is an ordinary event
that demands an extraordinary celebration.
What celebration,
to know that Jesus
is on the steps.

I am the way . . .
John 14:6

Mary's heart fell
and her spirit drooped
like a plant in early frost.
Old Simeon said
that her heart would be pierced
as with a sharp sword,
and she knew it.
Her spirit was to be prepared
for another temple visit
when he would be twelve,
and she would hold his strange sayings in her heart,
and when he was thirty
at a wedding in Cana
he would be more than son.
Jesus was her Lord.
And her spirit was prepared
for when he would be thirty-three
and she would go to Jerusalem
to his execution
and there carry spices
to his grave.
Her heart would hang there
to be revived.

But Mary kept all these things,
pondering them in her heart . . .
Luke 2:19

Herod was on a rampage
over the birth
of the Christ Child.
His men
searched in every direction,
winding through back roads
and charging down main streets
and searching out caves and houses
to seek the Child
among the Bethlehemites.
The rampage ended
in death —
the death of Herod.
Those who set out
to capture Christ
have their reward
in exhaustion
and self-destruction.
Children died.
Herod died.
The soldiers have died.
Christ lives.
Lord,
redeem man
from the exhaustion
that comes with destruction
and the careless rampage
against God's Son.

*Then Herod, when he saw
that he had been tricked by the wise men,
was in a furious rage . . .*
Matthew 2:16

There were in the temple
the aged.
Old Anna,
and old Simeon.
They were righteous
and devout
and in the Holy Spirit.
He came into the temple
and blessed God
and saw Jesus.
She came into the temple
and thanked God
and saw Jesus.
All who are old in the Spirit
praise God,
give thanks,
and then they see Jesus.

Simeon blessed them . . .
Luke 2:34

We saw the star
and have come from the East
to worship
the King.
They did not know
of the Child
born in hay.
They came to Jerusalem
to the palace
to seek a Child
in splendor
and in fine linen
and silk —
not there.
Again the star led them
from Jerusalem,
south
through the country,
past pastures
and around rocks and boulders
to a house
where the Child
was King
of kings.
There are stars
by which God points believers
to hiding places.

Lo, the star,
which they had seen in the East,
went before them . . .
Matthew 2:9

The Child grew
and lived by grace
on the way of life
that leads from heaven to earth
and to everlasting life.
By the narrow margin
of life or death
which holds all men to him,
he too lived
precariously,
in a day and land
of disease, leprosy.
No miracle drugs.
No aspirin.
No radium.
He was in all points
as man.
The grace of God
was upon him,
and he grew,
was strong in spirit,
and full of good knowledge.
Stem, bud, blossom, leaves,
joined
by the thin line of salvation
wherein the invisible will of God
threads time and space
and man
and God
together.

*Jesus increased in wisdom
and in stature . . .*
Luke 2:52

The Spirit
descended upon Jesus
like a dove,
and the voice from heaven
wove him into the godhead
saying, You are my beloved Son.
You please me.
The wilderness
was next,
and the temptation,
and the devil,
and hunger, and thirst, and wild beasts;
and the remembrance
of the Father's voice
and the dove.
Angels ministered to him.
There is always a way out,
even in the wilderness
with the devil,
to the one who
remembers the Spirit.

Thou art my beloved son . . .
Mark 1:11

Jesus said,
My kingdom
is not of this world.
He was
in the beginning
unraveling space and time
and form
and motion
and fire and water
and earth
and man.
In him
all things were created
in heaven,
on earth,
visible,
invisible,
and all power
and glory
and kingdoms.
The motion of the creation,
simple
and complex.
The motion of redemption
is also.

He is before all things . . .
Colossians 1:17

And they brought their children
to Jesus
and he blessed them.
Hope
is in the bud.
Fulfillment
is in the blossom.
Expectancy
is in the bud.
Fulfillment
is in the blossom.
Desire
is in the bud.
Fulfillment
is in the blossom.
The promise
and the secret
and the wonder
are locked in the bud.
Fulfillment
is in the flower.
And Jesus said,
Be as your children,
and you will be in my kingdom.
God's people
have hope, expectancy, promise, secrets,
and the fulfillment.
A man cannot return
to the bud
or to his mother's womb,
but he can be reborn.

Truly, I say to you, whoever does not receive
the kingdom of God like a child shall not enter it . . .
Mark 10:15

They brought
the diseased
to him,
and he healed them.
In that day
the waiting rooms
and surgeon tools
and communicable wards
were in front of Jesus
wherever he went.
Whether by the secret touching
of his garment
by a woman,
or by the bold imploring
of a father,
he was the Healer
in whom they believed,
or did not believe.
Some went away
healed
but unbelieving.
Others went away
healed
and believing.
Some leave
not healed,
only believing.

And he healed them . . .
Matthew 4:24

They waited for Jesus
to come from the mountain
where he had gone
to be glorified.
In the valley
the disciples wrestled with the mystery
and the power
of demons.
When Jesus came down
the mountain,
their faces were hopeful.
They waited
and watched
and stood amazed
as he defeated the demons
and healed the boy
immediately.
Transfiguration
had come down
into the valley.

Teacher, I beg you to look
upon my son . . .
Luke 9:38

Simon Peter
stood beautifully
before Jesus, saying,
I believe you are the Christ,
the Son of the living God.
There are times
when man is in full bloom
and unfolds every perfect piece of
heart and soul,
and Christ is Lord
and living God.
There are those times of day
and night
when man stands before the constant question
of Jesus,
But who do you say I am?
Then man either
shuts up
like blossoms at evening time,
or opens
as though before a full
sun.

*You are the Christ, the Son
of the living God . . .*
Matthew 16:16

Multitudes went before Jesus
and went after Jesus,
while many stood by,
asking
who this one in the street might be.
Their hurrahs
pointed heavenward
from every side
and from each heart.
It was a brief rehearsal
for their next cheer,
Crucify him.
The inconsistent anthem
of hurrah
and crucify
has a redeeming chorus —
Forgive them.
Father, forgive them.
He does.

All the city was stirred,
saying, "Who is this?"
Matthew 21:10

Come and drink,
all you little ones,
for Jesus is the water of life.
He quenches thirst.
He is the drink of salvation.
Take and drink,
for Jesus is the host
of a drink
of a vine
that has its roots in eternity
and its fruit on earth.
There are those dry places
quenched only
by love.
There is a thirst
that is more than parched throat,
and a drink
that is more than water.

*Whoever drinks of the water that I shall
give him will never thirst . . .*
John 4:14

He humbled himself
and was obedient
to die.
The crown of thorns
was before him
and where he knelt
he felt the curse
of Eden.
As he bent in prayer
to pull the curse up
by its roots,
they took thistles
and put them firmly
upon his head.
The thorns were long and hard;
the night was long and dark;
but the morning sun
was finally longer
and lighter.

*And plaiting a crown of thorns
they put it on his head . . .*
Matthew 27:29

And they all forsook him
and left him
alone
in the cold hands
of generation upon generation
of them that hate him.
He was held
in the fierce bite
of lies
and the eventual cold grip
of death.
In the leaders and soldiers
around him
merged all generations of men
before
and to come,
who forsake God
and join the army
and the jury of death
against the Prince
of life.
He understands
absolute
isolation.

*And they all forsook him,
and fled . . .*
Mark 14:50

In the water
they stood erect
and courageous
until they could not,
and by the blast of the north wind
were bowed to the water
and held there,
bent down,
frozen,
like winter bones.
The surface of Calvary
was as still
and solid cold
as frozen lakes
in the midst of a hard winter.
One nail held his feet
and two his hands,
and he stayed there
tight
until they loosed him
and took him down.
So it was too
with the two crucified
on either side.
They were at the mercy of the people,
and because of Jesus
under the mercy of the Father.

And they led him out
to crucify him . . .
Mark 15:20

On that dark day
two supporting crosses
stood on the hill
and he between them.
He
the first fruit,
like one lone timothy head
between two straight
blades of grass.
Between them
he hung
like full man
to deceive the captors
who were out to cut him down.
He is the fruit of the stem
and the seed of stalk.
who, when fallen to the earth
and into the earth,
proves before the eyes
of his captors
that good seed rises.
They crucified Jesus
between two thieves,
and on the third day
the Head of the church
was raised up,
a new Man.
He has promised
the victory of rebirth
to every man —
crucified,
dead,
and buried
and believing.

*Then two robbers were crucified
with him . . .*
Matthew 27:38

They found the grave empty.
The place where he had lain
held him
and could hold him no more.
His grave
became the pulpit
from which every sermon
is said.
The empty grave
has been lifted like a pulpit
in cathedrals,
in bronze
and marble
and wood,
and from it
the declaration of everlasting life
has been said
by memory
and by heart,
by orators
and by ordinary men.
From the pulpit
comes the message
about deep and distant places
in time
and in eternity.

Then go quickly and tell his disciples
that he has risen from the dead . . .
Matthew 28:7

Hearts can be heavy.
Two disciples
were on the road to Emmaus,
and their hearts
were weighted with disappointment
and the heaviness
of broken promises
and bent purposes.
Jesus came to them
and walked with them,
interpreting,
and listening
and eating,
until the weight was lifted,
their eyes opened,
and they saw Jesus.
When heavy hearts take a walk,
he walks along
until they can walk alone.

*While they were talking . . . Jesus
himself drew near . . .*

Luke 24:15

As men and women
reflected upon the resurrection
there was a sound
from heaven
like the rush of a great wind.
There appeared
tongues
like fire,
resting on each of them
who reflected.
The Man on the tree
had risen,
ascended,
and was in heaven.
The hour had come
for his promise to be kept,
and he kept it.
He sent the Spirit.
The autumn wind
and the leaves coming down,
and swirling
and resting finally somewhere,
are a colorful reminder
in the autumn
of the spring festival —
Pentecost.
The Spirit comes
in reflection
and meditation
upon the resurrection.

And suddenly a sound came from heaven
like the rush of a mighty wind . . .
Acts 2:2

And they stood
looking up into heaven
to see Christ
ascend
in the cloud.
The heads
and the hearts
of faith-filled men
are erect
and look ahead
by hope
the way they looked back
by faith.
To believe
and to hope
is to be elegant,
noble,
and to be straight.
Stand up,
for Jesus was here,
will come,
and he is here.

This Jesus . . . will come in the same way
as you saw him go into heaven . . .
Acts 1:11

The pod was broken,
and the seed was on its mission
of distribution.
The Holy Spirit was descended
and the lull and waiting were broken.
The story was released.
The news was out
on a mission of proclamation.
For each man
each day
is like the first descending of the Spirit
and the new mission
of distribution,
of proclamation.
The pod is broken,
while the next waits in line.

But you shall receive power when the Holy
Spirit has come upon you . . .
Acts 1:8

There are mansions above
to which men hold
by faith.
There is a life
that holds close
to an old story
of Jesus.
Though men live free
and move their own way,
they do not go far from the point
of the old story.
He has prepared a way
for man to go.
A way by which he will return.
On that road
man shall meet him.
It is a living
route.

And when I go and prepare a place for
you, I will come again . . .
John 14:3

There is for the spider
from its birth
a plan
whereby he patterns his daily work.
In each new web
the orbed threads
and spiral strands
are laid according to plan.
There is for man
from birth
a plan
whereby God patterns carefully
his daily life.
Man can break the design
of the Lord
for himself.
God's will is that man be saved
and know the truth.
According to plan
Jesus came
to do the will of the Father
in heaven.
The design
is clearly described
in a good Book.

I am the way, and the truth,
and the life . . .
John 14:6